My Brother's Book

Jack and Guy, two brothers, dreaming the same dream

My Brother's Book

Maurice Sendak

Michael di Capua Books

HarperCollins Publishers

Foreword

"A sad riddle is best for me," says Guy, stranded in Bohemia and desperately trying to keep from being eaten bite by bite by an enormous bear; "I have a winter one of long, long ago." Long ago indeed: *The Winter's Tale*, which haunts Maurice Sendak's imagination in his beautiful valedictory book, was written some four hundred years ago. Here, accompanied by exquisite pictures in the manner of Fuseli or Blake, pieces of Shakespeare's late romance are absorbed, redistributed, and transformed into something rich and strange. Shakespeare's doomed little boy, Mamillius, tells his mother that "A sad tale's best for winter." "I will tell it softly," he whispers, "Yon crickets shall not hear it." "Come on then," urges his mother, "and give't me in mine ear." "I'll whisper it," Sendak's Guy tells the bear; "the minutest cricket shall not hear." "Come on then! Give it quick in mine ear!" growls the bear. The play's frightening father has disappeared, displaced by the menacing embrace of an overpowering creature "Who hugged Guy tight / To kill his breath."

In Maurice Sendak's visionary worlds—widely recognized as among the greatest imaginative creations of our age— love often takes the form of menace, and safe havens are reached, if they are reached at all, only after terrifying adventures. Throughout his career and most intensely here, in his final expression of longing to be reunited with his dead brother, Jack, Sendak seems to have taken upon himself the challenge articulated by one of Shakespeare's characters: "a wild dedication of yourselves / To unpathed waters, undreamed shores."

—Stephen Greenblatt

My Brother's Book

On a bleak midwinter's night

The newest star!—blazing light!

So crystal bright!—eclipsing the moon,

Scorching the sky,

Smashed!—and heaved the iron earth in two,

Catapulting Jack to continents of ice—

A snow image stuck fast in water like stone.

His poor nose froze.

While Guy wheeled round in the steep air,
A crescent in the sky,
Passing worlds at every plunge—
Dropping down and down
On soft Bohemia

Into the lair of a bear

Who hugged Guy tight

To kill his breath

And eat him—bite by bite.

GUY

Answer my riddle and I will give you my life!

BEAR

Very well, a merry or a sad riddle shall it be?

GUY

A sad riddle is best for me.

I have a winter one of long, long ago—

I'll whisper it—the minutest cricket shall not hear.

BEAR

Come on then! Give it quick in mine ear!

SO BEGAN GUY

In February it will be

My snowghost's anniversary,

Jack's nose adrift in polar air,

Five years in iced eternity.

Bear!—Tell me!—Whither?—Where?

"To hell with you then!" the bear uproared,
Shadowing the sky, bellowing up a whirlwind
And slanting wide the world to the winter side—
And with his mighty paws scattering himself
Into a diadem of noble stars
Befitting Ursa Major.

Guy slipped dutifully into the maw of the great bear,

Diving through time so vast—sweeping past paradise!

Dissolving—all—into springtime

Where through the softly altered air

Guy listened to the meadow bird's solemn song.

A boy in winter fell deep in ice
And his dear nose froze.
Deep roots became his living toes.
For five long years he lay so sunk
Till bark enclosed his living trunk,
Bare vines entwined his glittering head.
Ask of the wild cherry tree:
Does he live? Is he dead?

And Guy sank upon a couch of flowers
In an ice-ribbed underworld
Awash in blossoming gold from a new sun
Tumbling out dark long-ago clouds,
Its caverns and corridors paved with painted petals
Wound round a wild cherry tree dusted pink.

Guy saw Jack's nose and rooted toes

Deep-buried in veiled blossoms

And he bit that nose—to be sure.

"Just lost—when I am saved!" Jack sighed.

And his arms, as branches will,

Wound round his noble-hearted brother,

Who he loves more than his own self.

And Jack slept safe,

Enfolded in his brother's arms.

And Guy whispered, "Good night

And you will dream of me."